The Diary of
Kiyoshi Tokutomi

translated by

Tei Matsushita Scott

with an introduction
and historical annotations by
Patricia J. Machmiller

Published by the Yuki Teikei Haiku Society
6116 Dunn Avenue, San Jose, CA 95123
www.youngleaves.org

Copyright©Tei Matsushita Scott, 2010

Second Edition

All rights reserved.

ISBN: 978-0-557-65437-6

Introduction
Kiyoshi Tokutomi: A Personal Memory

I meet Kiyoshi and Kiyoko Tokutomi in 1975 at the haiku workshop they conducted once a month in the San Jose Sumitomo Bank's Community Room. He was completely deaf when I met him, and I have to say that it was not difficult to communicate with him. I don't think any of his students found communicating with him difficult although he never learned sign language or lip reading. Generally, we communicated with him by the exchange of written messages. At the meetings his wife, Kiyoko, would sit beside him and as the discussion progressed, she would keep him apprised by ghost-writing Japanese/Chinese characters in the air with her right hand using her left palm and forearm as an imaginary tablet. Japanese is written from top to bottom, as you know. They were both bilingual in written and oral Japanese and English. If a subject or issue arose that he wanted to make a point about or comment on, he would speak up. If he was interrupting, Kiyoko would quietly put her arm on his, and he would stop; then when there was a break, she, or others, would indicate that now was the time to speak.

To give a little background: when Kiyoshi was eight (he was born in the U.S.), his father died. His mother sent his older sister, his younger brother, and him to Japan to be cared for by her family while she stayed in the U.S. to work. He was just finishing high school when the war broke out, and he was trapped in Japan. The conditions for civilians were very poor—no food or medicine; it was then he contracted tuberculosis. When he returned to the U.S., he was hospitalized for a long period of time. He lost one lung and half of the other so he was very weak. At some point he was given kanamycin for pneumonia that had the side effect of making him totally deaf. When he and Kiyoko learned that there was nothing to be done to restore his hearing, they decided that they would deal with the fact of his deafness as best they could. She had studied haiku in Japan (where she was born) as a young woman, and she thought that he might be interested in writing haiku. So she took him to a meeting of haiku writers in San Jose who were writing in Japanese. He was very excited about writing haiku and on the way home he said to her he thought English-speaking people would be interested in learning haiku. And so he began a yearlong study of haiku ordering books from Japan and filling his days with reading. As I said, he was very weak and really could not work. The effort to lift his arms to type on his typewriter was a strain; he could sustain it only an hour or so at a time. Writing in longhand was easier. He used long, yellow legal pads and wrote with a pencil.

I collaborated with Kiyoko and Kiyoshi doing translations. The way we would work is he would write out a literal translation of the article in longhand on these long yellow sheets and give them to me. I would then go through the text and make a second draft. Then we would sit together in my dining room or theirs and go over my draft word by word. I would ask questions in writing if I had not understood something. If he didn't like my word choice or if I had gotten the meaning wrong, he would tell me. I would offer alternatives in writing, and he would choose. Kiyoko sat between us and if we had difficulty communicating—this happened mostly in translating haiku—she would translate what I was saying into Japanese and air-write it on her palm. We had some very lively arguments in this three-way style. And then it the heat of the debate, it might be Kiyoko who would find just the right nuance that we were struggling for.

As a result of this translation work, I learned how sensitive the Japanese are to the rhythm of five-seven-five. Kiyoshi was adamant that we bring the haiku into English in five-seven-five form—it was extremely important to him. He did not like having to sacrifice the form, the rhythm, in the translation process. He would tap the rhythm out on the table as we worked.

The Tokutomis came to my house for socializing. They always enjoyed coming for Thanksgiving dinner. He never had any trouble communicating during dinner with my two teen-age sons and my husband. He seemed to know the rhythm of conversation and when to insert his comments. We always had a small pad of blank paper at the table so that people could respond to him by writing on the tablet and pass a note to him. Of course, Kiyoko sat beside him and would use her ghostwriting technique if necessary, but that usually wasn't required. One time we were having a party hosting the Tokutomis' best friends from Japan, the Naotsukas, and my mother happened to be here. She had meet the Tokutomis a few times on her visits to California, but had not interacted with them that much. During this particular party, she and Mr. Tokutomi were exchanging a long series of notes. All of a sudden there was uproarious laughter coming from the two of them. When the rest of us asked what was so funny, they dragged out the notes they had been exchanging and arranged them in order and read them out loud so the rest of us could share the joke! It is an example of how easily he fit into all situations.

He had a great sense of humor and a real zest for life. He appreciated the smallest things—being able to walk around the block, sitting in the shade in his yard in the summertime, making a Japanese "burrito" for anyone who came to call—like myself. In September 1978 I became the president of the Yuki Teikei Haiku Society, and as such, I often would go to his house to consult with him. If Kiyoko wasn't there, we would communicate entirely by writing—exchanging notes. Sometimes we would work through lunch, and he would offer to make something for us to eat. That's how I was treated to a Japanese "burrito"—Japanese leftovers wrapped in a tortilla!

As you will see from his diary, he kept up a large correspondence usually handwriting his letters. He also started the *Haiku Journal,* the annual publication of the Yuki Teikei Haiku Society, and *GEPPO,* Yuki Teikei's now bi-monthly newsletter. When he started it, it was sent out monthly. The format included poems from the members published anonymously, which then were voted on and the votes along with the names were published the following month. The *GEPPO* required a considerable amount of typing which he could not sustain. And so he recruited C. Joy Haas to edit it.

Even though he was greatly debilitated—diminished lung capacity, weakened upper body muscles, no ability to hear—he was always cheerful and optimistic. He lived his life to the fullest extent possible and took joy from small things. I feel privileged to have been able to learn from him, not just haiku, but how to live with grace and gratitude.

PATRICIA J. MACHMILLER

当用日記
1975
博文館

(July–December)

July 3

- In the evening Mammy and I visited Walstrand[1] to talk about haiku.
- Yukiko and Victor cut the grass.

[1]This would be Myron Wahlstrand of San Jose, CA. In August 1975 he and his wife hosted the first meeting the English Language Division of the Yukuharu Haiku Society which would ultimately become the Yuki Teikei Haiku Society. See Kiyoshi's entry on August 22.

July 4

Independence Day

- Kei-san came with his family.
- Mommy took Yukiko to see the fireworks.
- I'm not feeling well.

Aug 6

- Mommy came to the hospital in the morning to tell me about the meeting in Hawaii which she attended.
- Kei-san and his wife also attended and had told me about it. Mommy came right after that.
- I'm going to take penicillin again.

Aug 7

- Came home from the hospital. So good to be home!
- Mommy was going to take the proof-read patent[1] to Betsford. But decided to wait till tomorrow because it was getting late.

[1] Kiyoshi was working on in invention to be used in an automobile.

Aug 20

- Yukiko goes to Watsonville with her aunts.
- Received a letter from Shutō-sensei (he taught me at Shihan-gakkō). He is coming to the U.S. to attend a conference on history.
- My stomach is okay, but I cough too much . . . it's like an asthmatic attack.
- Kei-san came. I told him I will write an article on the Hawaiian Conference.

Aug 21

- Mommy took a day off.
- I wrote a report on the Hawaii Conference; had Mommy edit it and deliver it to Kei-san.
- Kei-san will edit it right away and mail it in the morning.

Aug 22

- Mommy, Susan[1], and I attended a haiku meeting at Mr. Wahlstrand's house.[2] It was a good gathering.
- I'm glad I met David.[3]

[1] Susan Soss
[2] This would be the first meeting of what would become the Yuki Teikei Haiku Society.
[3] David Earl McDaniel, retired librarian and president of the Friends of the Library Association.

Aug 23

- After dinner Mommy and I went to a haiku meeting (*kukai*[1]).
- On the way to the *kukai* we picked up Yukiko at the Greyhound Bus Station. She was in Watsonville.

[1] This was probably a meeting of the Japanese-language Yukuharu Haiku Society.

Aug 30

- Mommy and I went to buy cardboard for a windmill rib. Glad to find a compass there.
- Susan came.
- Kei-san came also, but he came on foot. I drove them home.
- Susan brought *uikyō* (fennel). It was very tasty.

Aug 31

- Rested all morning.
- I started the design of the rib for a windmill. Mommy helped me too.

Dill in a bottle
by the spiral-like windmill
on making table   [original in English]

Sept 6

- This morning I went to get tofu and made tofu-*misoshiru*.
- Prepared a collection of season words for October and took it to Susan for the *kukai* (haiku meeting).
- Her haiku is getting much better. The *kukai* is improving too.
- Too bad I couldn't find a ball bearing.

Sept 7

- Went to San Jose Library for a poetry meeting. Introduced the Yukuharu Haiku Society, and it was a great success. Together with Mommy we opened the meeting and each of us presented two haiku.[1]
- Mommy reported the above to Kei-san.

[1] It was at the San Jose Main Library on San Carlos Street. Patricia J. Machmiller was in the audience.

Sept 8

- Mommy took vacation time off.
- Sears came and installed a washing machine.
- Tube change at Dr. Higashi's. It was so painful that I had an injection afterward.
- Manuscript of haiku arrived from Motoyama Gyokushu-sensei.[1]
- Found the right ball-bearing for my use. Feel relieved.

[1] Gyokushu Motoyama edited the *Hawaiian Saijiki* for the Yukuharu Haiku Society's Hawaiian Division.

Oct 1

- Started to rewrite the application to Japan for a permit on the windmill.
- Forgot that today was the first Wednesday which is the day for English haiku. Kei-san let me know.
- It was a very nice meeting.

Oct 2

- Rested the whole day.
- Started to prepare for the design of the next generator.
- Prepared the package of haiku to send to Motoyama-sensei. Attached a letter.

Oct 3

- My 52nd birthday.
- Toshiko-san, my older sister, and three of us went to a Chinese restaurant to celebrate. Stopped at my brother's house after that.
- I was surprised to see Yukiko-san home.[1] She said she was studying hard. She said she had come home to sleep. I was impressed by her.
- I went to the machine shop, but the stuff I ordered had not arrived yet. I was disappointed.
- Went to the lumberyard to get some material for the next project.

[1] Yukiko is twenty and attending the University of California, Santa Cruz.

Oct 4

- Mommy went to the Japanese Language School.
- California Yukuharu Haiku Society meeting started at 6:30 p.m. I was so happy to see Tsukiji-san[1] there. Susan, Johnny[2], and we two [Kiyoko and Kiyoshi], the four of us made an English-language haiku group.
- After the meeting Kei-san treated us to ramen.
- Later Toshihiko-san came with a battery charger. We talked till after 2 o'clock.

[1] Eiichi Tsukiji, owner of Nikō Restaurant.
[2] This may be John Hickock. He was a neighbor of the Tokutomis when they lived on Eighth Street which is where they were living by this time. He was an early member of the Yukuharu English Language Division.

Oct 25

- Mommy taught in Japanese Language School; then went to work in the afternoon.
- Picked up the car, went to the lumberyard, picked up Mommy, and went to Fujimi-san's to have holes made in the wood.
- Manuscript finished. Mailing and delivering done. Sent one to Ochi-san and one to Kuwata-san. Tanaka-san is not home.
- I'm very tired and feel driven into the corner being so close to the close of day.

Oct 26

- Went grocery shopping.
- I went to get a calculator, but the shop was closed.
- I wanted to eat out with Kei-san and his wife, but they were not home. They stopped over at our house after eating out and surprised us.
- Mommy and I ate dinner at Okayama.

Nov 1

- Mommy worked at the Japanese school.
- Had a meeting of English-[language] Haiku at Sumitomo Bank. Twenty people attended. It was a successful *kukai*.
- Everybody liked Kei-san's presentation.
- Invited Ochi-san for dinner and went to the Champagne (?) Restaurant.

Nov 2

- Attended English-language poetry reading at the San Jose Library. I presented two of my haiku; Mommy recited winter haiku by Shūōshi. Everybody liked it.
- In the morning Mommy went to a gathering picking chestnuts; Daddy was getting ready to go to the library in the afternoon.
- Cooked chestnut rice and took it to Kei-san's office. Invited everybody on the second floor to lunch.
- Had dinner at Nikō Restaurant with Kei-san.
- Went to bed early.

Nov 3

- Reported to Tomotake-sensei about the past Saturday and Sunday.
- Prepared a speech on haiku which I am scheduled to give at the Poets' Association[1] to be held on the ninth.

[1] Most likely the Robert Frost Chapter in San Jose of the Chaparral Poetry Association of California.

Nov 28

- Mommy took a day off.
- Went to the Sumitomo Bank to make copies of haiku.
- Distributed copies to Kei-san, Kuwata-san, Tanaka-san, Ochi-san. To everyone else I sent copies by mail.
- Feel a bit tired.
- Mailed the manuscript and a letter to Motoyama Gyokushu-sensei.

Nov 29

- My mother-in-law sent us tea, seaweed, and pickled plums.
- Went to Mr. McDaniel's and Mr. Wahlstrand's to get the answers to the questionnaire.

Nov 30

- Akira-san[1] and his friends stopped over after seeing Glen-*chan*[2] to the airport.
- I had udon for lunch.
- Susan came. She stayed for my udon dinner. Also Yōzō-*kun*[3] stayed for dinner.
- Yukiko went back to school.
- I asked Susan to make a clean copy of the questionnaire and the answers so that it is easy to read.

[1] Akira Tao, husband of Kiyoko's sister, Mitusyo. He was a strawberry farmer in Watsonville.
[2] Glen Tao, oldest son of Mitsuyo and Akira Tao. *–chan* is a Japanese suffix indicating a young person.
[3] Yōzō Naotsuka came to live with the Tokutomis when he was going to high school. His parents were good friends of the Tokutomis, and they thought he needed a change of environment. He is now in college. The parents live in Tokyo. Mr. Naotsuka runs an export business. *–kun* is a Japanese honorific for a young adult.

Dec 1

- Started to write an article for the New Year's edition[1].
- Went to Mrs. Wass' house to collect the answers.

[1] Possibly *Hokubei Mainichi*, a San Francisco newspaper in Japanese.

Dec 4

- Mommy was so tired that she took a day off from work.
- Worked on a clean draft of the article for the New Year's edition.
- I gave a talk on the kigo [haiku season word] at McDaniel's.
- Went to Mrs. Hisakawa to pick up papers on mathematics.[1]
- Wrote a letter right away to the Education Committee of Okayama City.

[1] Kiyoshi and Kiyoko started a mathematics competition in the local grade schools and middle schools between Japan and the United States as a way to encourage young people in the study of mathematics.

Dec 5

- Completed the article for the New Year's edition.
- Prepared for the English language haiku meeting to be held tomorrow.

Dec 6

- Mommy worked at the Japanese Language School
- I left home for the English language haiku meeting which was to start at 1:30 p.m.
- Fifteen attendees—it made me very happy. It looks like the foundation has been set now.
- Had dinner at Okayama together with Susan.
- Attended *kukai* in Japanese. Mommy joined me after attending a meeting of the teachers at the Japanese Language School.
- I'm tired of the meetings.
- I was told that Yukiko came home about 11:00 a.m.. We went to McDonald's as she wanted.

Dec 7

- Rested until noon.
- Had forgotten about the presentation at the Poets' Society [Robert Frost Chapter]. Went there in a hurry.
- Took Yukiko and Valery to Eastridge [Shopping Mall].
- I went to bed early because I was very tired.

当用日記
1976
博文館

Jan 2

- Mommy prepared a treat to entertain Mr. Miyagi and his group from Japan Airlines who are coming tomorrow.
- After dinner we made New Year's calls to Yoshimitsu-san[1] and Yamamoto-san.
- Toshikiko-san came. We talked about motors. He gave me a switch.

[1] Yoshimitsu is Kiyoshi's younger brother.

Jan 3

- While I was cooking chicken unexpectedly I found the solution for the AC motor. It made me very happy.
- Regular meeting of English haiku was a great success.
- Onodera-san and Makita-san came to see me. (Miyaji-san couldn't come because of a test.)
- After dinner we attended a regular meeting of Japanese haiku.

Jan 4

- Got up at 10:30 a.m. Mommy got up early and prepared *mochi-*soup and breakfast.
- Onodera-san and Makita-san joined us.
- Took them to the Tanaka's house to see their carnation hot house.
- Took them to the airport.
- Took goodies to my sister. Saw Grandmother. I was surprised to find that she was in good shape.

Jan 5

- Prepared to print the questions in the mathematics contest. I was told that Takeda-san will come on the day of the contest.
- Prepared an article for the newspaper on the mathematics contest.
- Memberships for English haiku (Mrs. [Bohumila] Falkowski, Mrs. [G. Clary] Adams, Mr. [Hal] Dumas, Susan—$13 for 6 months).

Jan 8

- Yōzō-*kun* returned to the U.S.
- I feel relatively energetic.
- Mommy cleaned the porch.
- Yōzō-*kun* wants to come this evening, but we decided to delay it till tomorrow because I am tired. We'll have dinner together.
- Mommy and I went to Sumitomo Bank and thanked Mr. Kimura, the branch chief, for their help.

Jan 9

- I have a headache due to lack of sleep.
- The invitation to the mathematics competition was written with the help of Hirabayashi branch chief.
- [Kiyoshi's writing unclear here].
- Membership fees for the English Haiku Club totals $88.00.
- Preliminary talks on the New Year's party took place at Kei-san's house. Tanaka-san was there too.

Jan 14

- A thank-you note was sent with the invitation to the Education Bureau.
- No application yet—makes me disappointed. I'm going to call Tsuji-san and Hirakawa-san[1]. Hirakawa-san said that the invitation would arrive today, but Tsuji-san has not received it yet.
- Prepared the proof of English haiku written by the members which is to be sent to Japan.
- Yōzō-*kun* came to see me.
- An electric blanket seems to be harmful to the heart.

[1]Hirakara was the President of the Yukuharu Haiku Society of Japan. He lived in Tokyo.

Jan 15

- Finished the certificates for English haiku written by the members to be sent to Japan. Wrote a letter to Hirakawa-sensei.
- Went to see Mr. McDaniel together with Mommy to confer on season words. Took the dictionary of Kenyū-sha which Mr. McDaniel wanted to have.
- English haiku was sent to Japan just in time.
- How greedy man is . . . to wish for heavenly treatment.
- Great inventions and discoveries are not realized only by genius. If they were, there would be no excitement of discovery.

Jan 26

- Went to the hospital; inserted tubes twice.
- Headache. I hate the hospital.
- Mommy did not go to work.

Jan 27

- Mommy worked on haiku and haibun to send to Japan.
- Mommy left the hospital early in order to prepare haiku to be sent to headquarters in Japan.

Jan 30

- Removed the tube.
- I am to be released from the hospital.
- Found it difficult to walk.
- Yukiko and the daughter of the owner of the coffee shop, Brazil, came to see me.

Jan 31

- Mommy worked at the Japanese Language School.
- I was released from the hospital.
- Yōzō-*kun* came to take me home.
- Had to go back to the hospital immediately and put the tube in right away.

Feb 3

- Mathematics competition.
- Susan came; she went home because I was sleeping.

Feb 4

- Thank-you note to Mr. Kimura for the mathematics competition.
- Turned off the suction pump.
- Kei-san and his family came to see me.
- Mommy brought me weekly magazines.

Feb 5

- Mommy came to see me early.

Feb 6

- Tube removed.
- Susan came to see me. We talked for awhile.

Feb 7

- Wrote thank-you notes to Imazaki-san and Kurimura-san for the article.
- Had English haiku meeting first; then the Japanese.
- After the English haiku meeting I got a surprise visit from Mommy and Akira-san.
- Later Mommy came back alone to change my dressing.

Feb 8

- Mommy came around noon with English newspapers.
- Mr. [Edwin] Falkowski writes English haiku well.
- Mommy went to the Robert Frost poetry meeting.

Feb 9

- Released from the hospital. Mommy came to take me home at 2:15 p.m.
- Wrote a letter to Tomiyasu-san
- Susan came to see me.

Feb 10

- Mommy took a day off.
- Akira-san and family came to see me from Watsonville.
- Kei-san and his family came in the evening.
- Wrote an article on tofu-making machine for Kei-san.
- Kimura Branch Chief of Sumitomo Bank gave me a pot of beautiful flowers.
- Wrote a letter to Hirakawa-san.
- Began to translate haiku into English.

Feb 15

- Second haiku meeting.
- Akira-san's family came to see me.

the dawn is broken
with the first jump of the grass
hopper at the field   [original in English]

statue of the Buddha
eyes half closed
the spring breeze

fire engine
in the deserted street
birds chirping

Feb 16

- Worked on the statistics of the mathematics competition.
- Yukiko came home with Melanie from San Francisco.
- Mommy drove Yukiko to Santa Cruz.
- Wrote a letter to Hirakawa-sensei about the translation of English haiku into Japanese along with an explanation.
- Kei-san and his wife came to see us.

Feb 21

- Mommy taught at the Japanese Language School.
- Together with Mommy I visited Toshiko-san in his sick bed.
- Felt very tired; taken to the hospital because of a collapsed lung. Dr. Shizman put the tube in.
- I don't know what's going on.

Feb 22

- Moved to a different room downstairs.
- Taniguchi-san and Takeda-san came and discussed how to incorporate as a company.
- Mommy had a flat tire. Taniguchi-san took her to Union Tire to have it changed.
- She took Taniguchi-san and his son to Mandarin Restaurant for dinner.
- I was told that my backache is related to my collapsed lung. Now I understand.

Feb 23

- I had a terrible attack. Nobody came to help me. I thought this was the last. There was no room service or any way to get help. They quickly inserted the tube.
- Then they called the management office to change my room.

Feb 24

- Changed my room to upstairs again.
- Ishizeki-san and Yamada-san came. I am so grateful. They are nice people.
- I don't feel well. The doctors are busy with their operations until 11 o'clock.

Mar 1

- A letter arrived from the Education Committee of Okayama.
- The tube was removed.
- I transferred to a different room downstairs.
- I am surprised to find myself so weak.
- Mommy came at 6:30 p.m.

Mar 2

- Came home from the hospital.
- Had lunch at Nikō with Mommy. Mrs. Tsukiji gave us *inarizushi* [a rice ball in a thin coating of fried tofu].
- Mommy printed the manuscript of haiku and mailed it.
- Kei-san and his family came.
- I let Takeda-san know that I am home now.
- I reported the same to Dr. Keisler.
- Mommy wrote a letter to Okayama City's Educational Committee that the statistical data will be coming late.
- Asanazeki-san came to see me.
- Mr. Falkowski wants me to edit haiku of the All-America Competition.

Mar 3

- Mommy took a day off.
- She made a package for my mother and mailed it.
- A letter came from [Kiyoko's] Mother in Nabeshima, Japan. She says that Fukaya-*kun* is coming to the U.S. to go to the para-Olympics in Canada.
- Yōzō-*kun* came to see me.

Mar 6

- Mommy taught Japanese at the Japanese Language School.
- It was a successful English haiku meeting. Pat [Machmiller] became a member.
- There was a haiku meeting in Japanese; I feel tired.
- Ochi-san came to see me.
- From Mother-in-law . . .

Mar 7

- Went to the shopping center with Yōzō-*kun* to buy a plate to give to Mr. Wadensweiler.
- Prepared to get an amendment from Japan.
- Asked Mommy to make a clean copy.

Mar 18

- Went to see Dr. Higashi to change my tube. I was surprised to find that both my legs became numb. I am concerned with my heart. I am glad that I stopped taking tranquilizers. One should not take pills unless absolutely necessary.

Mar 19

- A letter from Izuka. He seems to be negotiating with Sony. I'm grateful.
- Wrote a letter to the Sumitomo Bank in Okayama about the mathematics contest.
- Wrote articles for the newspaper in Japanese and English.
- Mommy and I went to see Mr. McDaniel. Felt tired, but the drive made me feel better.

Apr 3

- Mommy worked at the Japanese School.
- George-san went home. We saw him to the airport.
- I feel lonely.
- Mommy and I went to see Tsujiki-san in the evening. It is so good to talk to him. He makes me relaxed.
- The meeting of English haiku started at 1:30 p.m. Sixteen people attended. It was great.

Apr 4

- Went shopping at the stationary [store]. Mommy was with me.
- Drove alone to Kei-san's.
- Imamura-san came to see me. We talked about Akizuki-san.

Apr 9

- Thought about a method that [uses] a radius-like coil for the single-pole-shield magnet.
- If so, the starting is solved with the rotating maximum torque.

4月9日　金曜

旧 3.10

- radius-like coil の方法を考えて、いよいよこれで成立するのか？

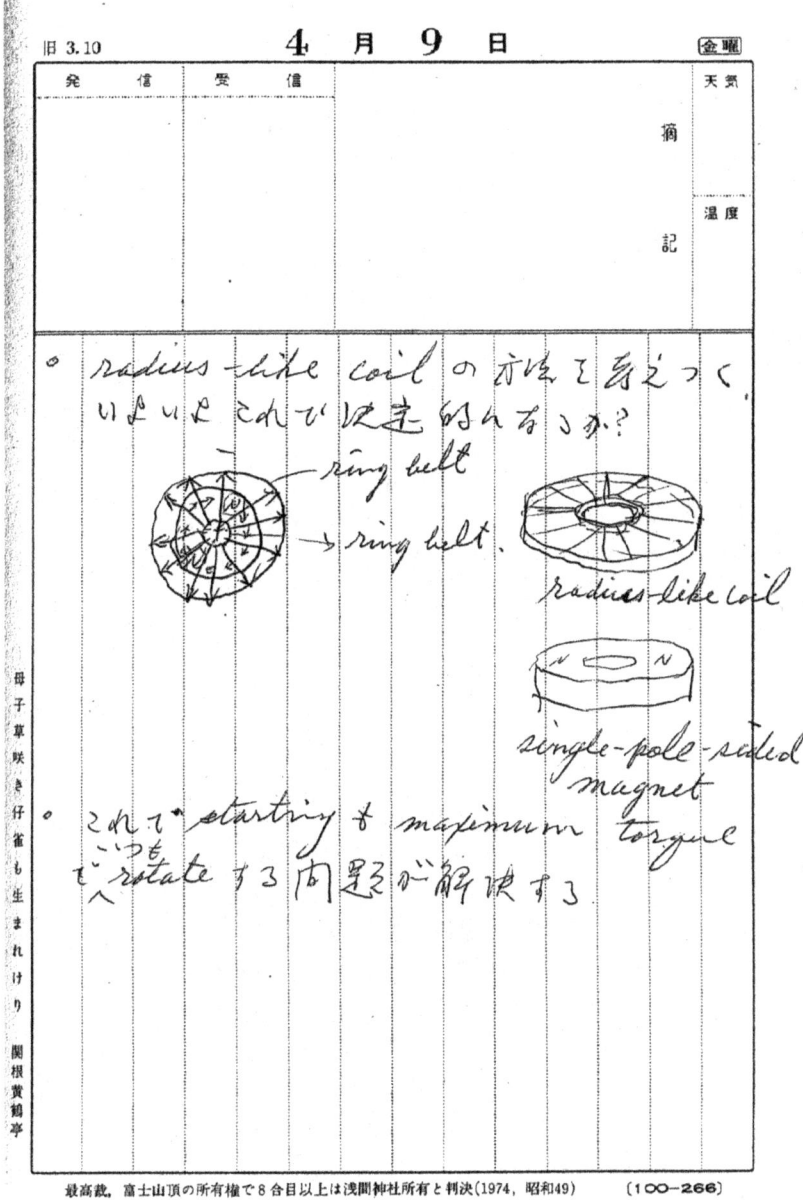

→ ring belt
→ ring belt
radius-like coil
single-pole-sided magnet

- これで starting も maximum torque で いつも rotate する問題が解決する

Apr 10

- Mommy taught at the Japanese School.
- I spent the afternoon thinking about the radius coil.
- There was the Japanese haiku meeting in the evening.
- Yamada-san came. I was so glad to see Toshihiko-san.
- After the *kukai* [haiku meeting], we stayed and talked to Kei-san's group.

Apr 11

- Takeda-san came at 10 o'clock in the morning. I explained the theory of the new radius-like coil showing him the design. We decided to make a simple sample.
- I asked Takeda-san to name this the one-sided pole.
- In the afternoon I attended a poetry reading at the Robert Frost [Poetry Group]. Mommy and Yukiko came too.
- In the evening I took Yukiko back to school in Santa Cruz.

Apr 12

- Translated the members' English haiku into Japanese. Wrote a patent application on the radius-like coil.
- After dinner went to Yamamoto-Suejo-san's house with Mommy. We were surprised to hear that Yamamoto-san had left the Yukuharu-*kai* [group] of San Jose.

Apr 17

- Takeda-san went to Fresno today. He might see Taniguchi-san there.
- Went grocery shopping.
- Kei-san invited us to a restaurant for dinner. Katayama-san will be there too.

Apr 18

- Went to Yamamoto-san's to see *sakura* [cherry blossoms] with double flowers.
- Haiku gathering. We went to Yamamoto-san's to see the double-flowering sakura.
- Akira-san's family came for dinner with their "uncle"—me.

Apr 21

- Translated Dr. [Edwin] Falkowski's article.
- It is in the weekly which is now in the stores. Bought the magazine and read the translation.

Apr 22

- All day I was thinking of the rotating magnet as shown in the drawing [see p. 34].
- I received a thank-you note from Kiyoko's parents. It was for the package we sent them.
- Mailed to Hirakawa-sensei an article titled "Easter and the California Poppy" written by Dr. Falkowski.

木曜		4 月 22 日		旧 3.23
発信	受信		天気	
			独記	
			温度	

○ 一日 rotating magnet について考える

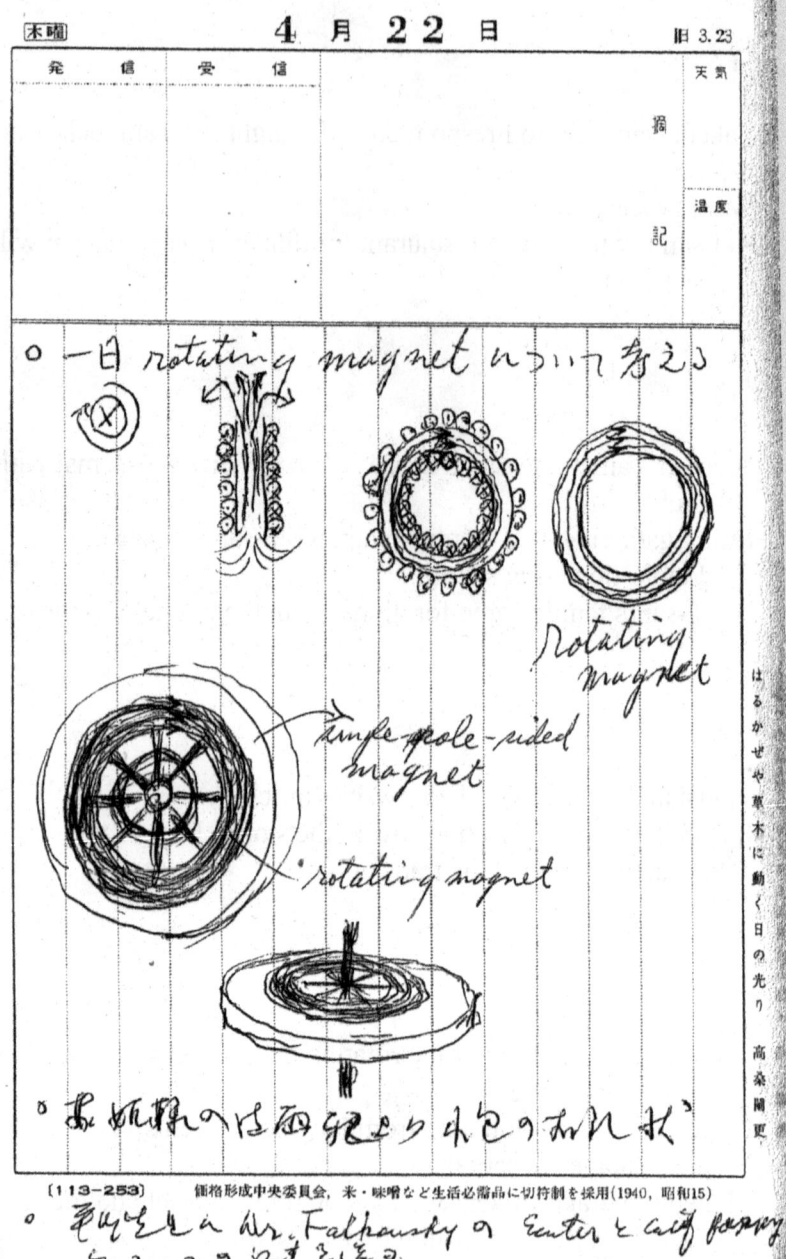

○ お姉様のは西紀より水色の小れんげ

[113-253] 価格形成中央委員会，米・味噌など生活必需品に切符制を採用(1940, 昭和15)

○ 兄上さんに Dr. Falkowsky の Easter と Calif poppy についての記事を送る

はるかぜや草木に動く日の光り 高桑闌更

May 1

- Mommy taught at the Japanese School.
- Had English haiku meeting from 1:30 p.m. It went very well. Kei-san attended and talked about the Yukuharu competition.
- Haiku meeting in Japanese in the evening.. There was an informal dinner to welcome new members.
- Akira-san's group came.

May 2

- 2:00 p.m. Went to the San Jose Library to attend a meeting of the Poets' Association.
- McDaniel-san said, "It's good to be old." He said, "For example, old folks remember the train." I agreed with him and recited my haiku in English:

moonflower blooming
at the side of the railroad track
no more steam engine   [original in English]

He was very pleased.

- Yamamoto-san's group came before noon.

June 4

- In the evening I asked Takeda-san to come, and we discussed the design of the parts shown [Kiyoshi has a sketch of the part]. We decided to make a sample.

June 5

- After lunch was the English haiku meeting.
- In the evening was the haiku meeting in Japanese. I had a headache. I don't know why my condition is unstable.
- Yamamoto's group joined the meeting; everyone enjoyed it.
- After the meeting Yamamoto-san's group came to our house,
- After the meeting, I went to the Notary office.
- I purchased a magazine in Japanese.

June 10

- Today is Paul's [Akira Tao's middle son] graduation day. Mommy came home around noon, and we went to the ceremony.
- Someone in charge of Social Welfare came.
- I feel uncomfortable with my stomach.
- Akira-san and his family took us to a restaurant.
- Yukiko came from Santa Cruz and waited for us in Akira-san's truck for more than two hours.
- I feel unsteady in the head because I didn't sleep well last night.
- Cannot stop thinking of the magnet. Wish I could find a solution to this problem.

June 11

- I couldn't sleep last night. Mommy said that in marriage one has to make the partner happy . . .
- Maybe I succeeded with the magnet. I didn't realize, but the ring magnet might work. I don't know why I didn't realize it before. I wonder if this will lead to a non-current motor.

| 金曜 | 入梅 (陰暦80度) | 6月11日 | 旧 5.14 |

|発信|受信| | 天気 |
| | | 簡記 | 温度 |

○昨晩ねむれでん聞いすか、そんな心力万 引を考えてねむれすかった。夫婦の委 "和も幸せんな義務がある"とマーで か一云ったか―

○どうせふ magnet の方は成功したかも知れ ない。全く気がつかなかった。Cuよっ とりと. 輪(?)で気んつく. この端のところを利用しないくて なんと、今後気付えたかったこと占.

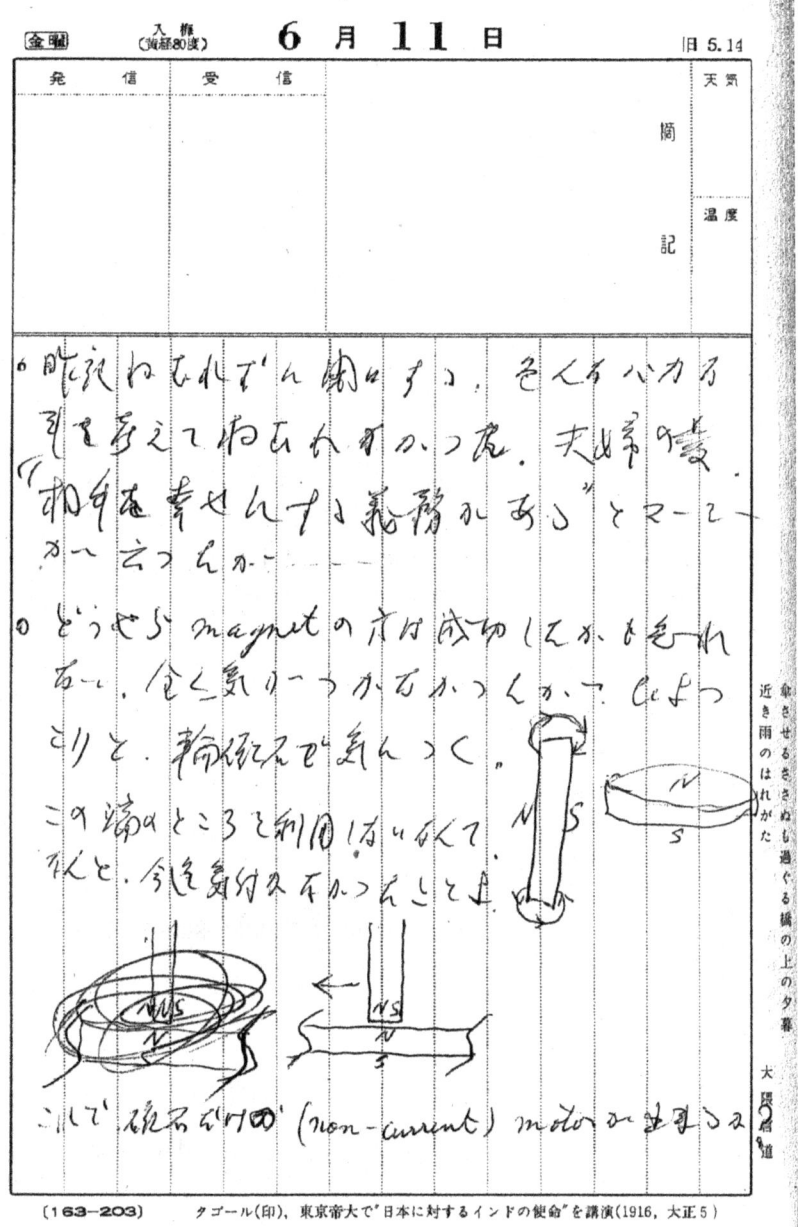

これで 磁石だけの (non-current) motor が出きる ?

July 2

- The son of Mrs. Yoshizumi and Mr. Iwashita came to see me. We talked about why their haiku club has spirit.
- I took a pain-killer instead of a sleeping pill last night but couldn't sleep. Instead I had a headache. I took ice water then. About 4:00 a.m. the headache was gone.
- Yukiko and Yumiko-san went to Big Basin. They took sleeping bags.

July 3

- It looks like Yukiko and her friends are going to spend another night in Big Basin.
- I asked Ishimatsu-san to come over, and Kei-san, and I tried to explain it to them. Kei-san was pleased.
- After dinner I attended the regular *kukai* at Kei-san's. I was awfully tired so I lay down on Kei-san's sofa-bed. The following is the haiku I made:

water basin . . .
stopping by for a second
a summer butterfly

- I came home early so that I can take Tanaka-san around tomorrow.

July 10

- Today was the English haiku [meeting]. Attendance was very small.
- Had dinner at Nikō Restaurant.

July 11

- The sedatives seemed to have worked.
- But I don't know what to do with the tube when it hurts.

Aug 7

- English haiku meeting.
- Japanese haiku meeting. Having two meetings made me exhausted.
- San Jose Yukuharu group is reported to have started a sign-up movement. It makes me really mad. They didn't discuss anything with us. What can I say . . . they are the type of people who do viscous things behind pleasant talk.

Aug 8

- Kei-san proposed to talk to Mr. Iwashita. Mr. Iwashita ducked the issue, recommending that we talk to Mr. Katayama.
- Kei-san reported the above to Ishimatsu-san.
- Mommy reported the above to Mr. Honda.
- I finished translating a letter from ?-sensei.
- Went to see Hisayo-san [Kiyoko's sister who was living in San Jose].
- I can't get the magnet out of my head.

Sept 4

- Regular meeting of English haiku.
- Rested.
- Mailed a clean copy of English haiku to Hirakawa-sensei.

Sept 5

- Presentation at Poets' Association. I sent in two haiku.
- Ōmari-san came to see us.
- Kei-san's group came too.
- I kept thinking of the magnetic motor.

Oct 2

- English haiku regular meeting. Thirteen people attended.
- I attended the Japanese *kukai* [haiku gathering]. Feel tired.
- After the meeting we talked about the Autumn Festival at haiku. Tanaka-san was there too.

Oct 3

- This is my birthday. I forgot.
- Susan came to see us.
- Together we went to Azuma [Restaurant].

Oct 10

- Attended the [Robert Frost] Poets' Association gathering with Mommy.
- After that Dr. Falkowski and I judges the entries of haiku from all over the country.
- Went to Fumihiko-san's to have a Chinese dinner. We took Yōzō-*kun* too.

Oct 11

- Columbus Day.
- Mommy went to work.
- After dinner we went to Hisayo-san's.
- Wrote a letter to Hirano-sensei. I sent him the selections from all the American haiku entries submitted yesterday.

Oct 16

- Mommy taught at the Japanese Language School.
- In the afternoon she went to San Francisco for a meeting of Japanese Language Schools' teachers.
- She came home at exactly six o'clock. I was surprised.

Oct 17

- The second regular meeting of haiku.
- At three o'clock Mommy has a meeting with Mr. Katayama and his group. How could one become so base? Mommy was disgusted with his scheming character. There is no need to continue our relationship.

Nov 5

- Regular meeting of the English haiku group.

Nov 6

- Attended [Robert Frost] Poets' Association meeting.
- Became a member of the World Poetry Society.
- Feel tired after attending both meetings.
- Went to Hoshinos' [Kiyoshi's sister, Mitsuye, and her husband].

Nov 13

- Mommy taught at the Japanese School.

Nov 14

- All-America Grand Meeting on Poetry.
- Kei-san accompanied me.
- Successful in translating into English
- Went to San Francisco together with Kei-san's group to meet Yamagata-san[1].

[1]Teruo Yamagata, member of the Yukuharu Haiku Society of Tokyo, Japan. He became a lifelong member if Yuki Teikei Haiku Society. Several years ago he became president of the Yukuharu Haiku Society with groups in Tokyo, Hawaii, and San Jose.

Nov 15

- Went to see a house.
- Wrote a letter to Hirakawa-san [President, Yukuharu Haiku Society, Tokyo].
- Wrote an article on the postponement of the Haiku Festival.

Nov 16

- Went to see a house.
- Plan to make a plaque.
- Went to see the doctor to have my tube changed.

Dec 1

- Wrote a letter to Mr. Ikari.
- Distributed copies of haiku.
- Went to see Kei-san.
- Wrote a letter to Hirakawa-sensei.
- Bulletin of the [Robert Frost] Poets' Association arrived. Very poor quality; trying to copy others.

Dec 2

- Wrote a letter to Hirakawa-sensei, but did not mail it.
- There was a phone call to Mommy from Dr. Frederika Blankner[1]. She wants to open a branch [haiku] office in New York. What good news!

[1] Frederika Blankner was listed as the East Coast Vice President, English Language Division, Yukuharu Haiku Society of Japan, in *Haiku Journal*, Vol. 1, 1977.

当用日記
1977

博文館

Jan 1 (cloudy)

- Got up at 11:00 in the morning.
- Our family of three and Yōzō-*kun* celebrated the New Year by having spiced sake and rice-cake soup.
- I needed more sleep. Feel tired. My back aches. Yesterday I helped prepare the rice-cake soup peeling potatoes, cutting chicken, etc. Maybe that's why I'm so exhausted.
- Wrote a New Year's message and also an article about the shortage of the water supply for a column in the San Jose News.
- Visited Edge Sayoko-san. She served us the New Year's Day cuisine and took pictures of us with a Polaroid camera. Came home about 11.
- Called the family in Japan around 5:00 p.m., but nobody was home.

Jan 2 (rainy)

- Got up at 11:00 a.m.
- We went to Watsonville. Glen-*chan* [the oldest son of Kiyoko's sister, Mitsuyo] will go back to school today.
- Stopped to see Hisayo-san. We watched TV and came home around 10:30 p.m.
- Had supper.

Feb 5

- Kiyoko seemed to have slept well by taking a tranquilizer.
- She went to the Japanese [Language] School.
- She went to the English haiku *kukai* and the Japanese haiku *kukai* alone.
- I stayed home because I didn't feel well.
- Susan came to take care of me while Kiyoko worked.
- Got a good idea about the windmill.

Feb 6

- Feel a little bit better. I'm relieved.
- It seems placing a stone on my chest works.

Feb 7

- I feel much better.
- Worked on the statistics of the mathematics contest.
- Wrote and article on it for the newspaper.
- Wrote a thank-you note to Junko-san[1].

[1] Junko House, member of the local Japanese Yukuharu group.

Feb 8

- I feel almost normal. Feel relieved.
- Kiyoko came home around noon.
- A man came to adjust the C.H. (?)
- After waiting for so long, a man finally came to put salt in the water softener.
- Worked on the statistics for the mathematics contest.
- I prepared hamburger for our dinner.
- [Received] a letter from Naotsuka.
- Yōzō-*kun* came.

Mar 3

- Wrote a letter to Ikari-*kei*[1].
- After dinner we went to see Hisayo-san.

[1] *kei* is a Japanese honorific showing respect to a man senior to the speaker.

Mar 4

- Prepared to translate January and February issues of English haiku to send to Japan.

Mar 5

- English haiku meeting.
- Japanese haiku meeting.
- Kiyoko worked at the Japanese [Language] School.
- Feel a bit tired.
- Purchased Japanese magazines *(Asahi Weekly, Sunday Mainichi, Bungei-Shunjū).*

A flock of pigeons
circling around the church dome
Spring is in the sky   [original in English]

Mar 6

- Attended [Robert Frost] Poetry Association meeting in the library.
- Wrote an explanation of the windmill.
- Visited Toshiko-san in his sick bed.

Mar 15

- Started to work on *Haiku Journal*.
- Susan came.
- Wrote a letter to Dr. Blankner.

Mar 16

- Received a letter from Miki-sensei (a member of the Okayama-shi Education Committee).
- Wrote a draft of a letter to the mayor of Okajaki-shi asking that the Education Committee join the festival that will commemorate their 200-year history.
- Yukiko came home without letting us know.
- Together with Kiyoko thought about Yukiko's future.
- Translated the syllabus of Hirakawa-sensei. Worked on *Haiku Journal*.
- Junko-san and Sayoko-san came with their haiku.

Mar 17

- Kiyoko stayed home due to a cold.
- Sent letters to Okazaki Hideo (mayor of Okayama-shi) and Miki-sensei.
- Crossed copper wire between north and south magnetic poles. Current will not flow (?) into copper wire, and it is confirmed that electricity flows when the current crosses from N to S.
- Thank you note to Junko-san.

Mar 18

- Postcard from Yamagata-san. He is not coming to the U.S.
- Translated Pat [Machmiller]'s Haiku News.
- After dinner we went to see my sister.

Mar 19

- Kiyoko worked at the Japanese [Language] School.
- Visited Yoshimitsu [Kiyoshi's younger brother].
- Kiyoko had a preliminary meeting at the Mt. View Buddhists' Association about the speech contest to be held tomorrow.
- Bought a lawn mower.

Mar 20

- Had a second regular meeting.
- Akira-san [Kiyoko's brother-in-law who was married to Mitsuyo] and his family came.
- Kiyoko went to the speech contest.
- Had dinner together with Akira's family.
- We went to see Hisayo-san and watched the TV broadcast in Japanese.

Mar 21

- Translated the synopsis of the history of Yukuharu.
- In the evening Kei-san and his wife came with a present for the new house.
- Kei-san and his wife made their selection of haiku to send in to the newspaper.
- Taniguchi-san phoned. He is coming on Friday.
- A signed check came from Dr. Falkowski (for sending the membership fee to Japan).
- Yamada-san came (with haiku).

Mar 22

- Motoyama-san's letter came with haiku.
- Thank-you note from Takasugi-san. I replied.

Apr 1

- Wrote English haiku
- Kiyoko came home about one hour earlier [than usual] due to a cold.
- Went to Ogura to buy books.
- Picked dandelions.

Shaving my face
you or I
must be a fool

I forgot
what I was talking about—
April Fool's Day

April Fool's Day—
I almost choke
on a drink of water

April Fool's Day—
I wrote on the envelopes
twice upside down

April Fool's Day—
eating porridge
I bit my tongue

April Fool's Day—
sprinkling birdseed
the sparrows flew away

April Fool's Day—
what I just learned
I've forgotten already

Apr 2

- Kiyoko went to the Japanese School but came home early due to her cold.
- Regular meeting of the English haiku group. Submitted five English haiku of which one received four points and one three points.
- Conferred with Dr. Falkowski about the *Yukuharu Journal (Haiku Journal?)*.
- Attended Japanese *kukai* in the evening.

Apr 3

- Stayed in bed in the morning.
- Went to see Tanaka-san because his greenhouse was damaged by a tornado. I was surprised to see that pieces of 2 x 4s were scattered all over the place. Tanaka-san thought that an airplane crashed into the area.
- In the evening Kiyoko and I attended the twentieth anniversary of Sakura Garden [a restaurant where Kiyoko once worked when she first came to America].
- On the way back home we stopped to see Hisayo-san.

Apr 4

- Received letters from Yamagata-san and Sugi-san.
- Wrote back to them right away.
- Wrote a letter to Hirakawa-sensei about the dues from the English haiku members.
- Kiyoko took time off in the morning and went to work in the afternoon.

Apr 17

- Second regular meeting of haiku.
- Akira-san and his wife [Mitsuyo, Kiyoko's sister] came to see us.
- The four of us went to see Hisayo [Kiyoko's other sister here in the U.S.].

Apr 18

- Prepared to teach haiku on the twentieth to Japanese-English education group.

Apr 19

- Sayoko-san and her husband came to see us.
- Prepared for tomorrow's event.

Apr 20

- Kiyoko and I went to Albert Elementary School in San Francisco to teach haiku.
- Kiyoko went to her hairdresser.

May 5

- I'm in pain. I don't want to do anything.

May 6

- The pain continues.

May 7

- Kiyoko went to the Japanese [Language] School.
- English haiku regular meeting. Torrential rain. Mr. [Ed] Thompson came with his haiku. It was about new shoots of pine. Good observation.
- Had the Japanese *kukai* in the evening. Kiyoko led the meeting very well.
- I took Demerol and aspirin in succession before going to the *kukai*. I didn't expect to become ill, but I did.

May 8

- Took a long rest.
- In the evening we went to my sister's to watch TV.

May 17

- A letter came from Fukaya-Kazumi-san. I was so grateful.
- Worked on English haiku.
- Wrote a letter to Taniguchi-san about how to make the windmill.
- Yōzō-*kun* came.
- Dinner, then a haircut.

May 18

- Wrote a letter to Kazumi-san.
- Worked on English haiku.
- In the evening went to Tsukiji-san's house and stayed about an hour. He showed me an album of photos from his younger days.

May 19

- A letter and the *Mainichi Newspaper* came from Takaha Shugyō-sensei[1]. I am so grateful and touched.
- I reported this to my wife. She came home for her lunch break.
- I am full of hope.
- I drafted a letter to Takaha-sensei.

[1] Shugyo Takaha is one of the leading haiku poets in Japan today. His haiku organization is Kari. Kiyoko and Kiyoshi became his students. In 1997 he elevated Kiyoko to *dojin,* a special designation given to advanced writers in Japanese haiku societies.

May 20

- Spent the day with hope and determination.
- Wrote a letter to Takaha-sensei.
- Asked my wife to edit the letter.

May 21

- Made a clean copy of the letter to Takaha-sensei and took it to the Main Post Office together with my wife.
- Went to Toshihiko-san's to borrow his Polaroid camera. I am going to make photos of Kelly Park for the newspaper.

May 22

- Kiyoko went to pick up Hisayo's group. I rested all morning to prepare for the afternoon.
- After lunch I went to Kelly Park to collect data for the newspaper. I had a successful interview with Mr. Moritaka (Assistant Chief of Administration).
- I attended the welcome-home party for Kei-san. There I heard about Hirakawa-sensei's resignation. I was shocked.
- Went to Hisayo-san's group with Akira-san's group.
- Wrote the article for the newspaper about the interview mentioned above.

May 23

- Wrote letters to Hirakawa-sensei and Motoyama-sensei. I am so tired!
- A letter came from Mori-san.
- I must work harder in the field of English haiku. I want to spend the rest of my life translating Takaha's book.
- I must study English.

May 24

- Went to see Dr. Higuchi.
- Yōzō-*kun* came to see us.
- Began to study English.
- Mailed the article on yesterday's interview.

May 25

- Studied English
- Wrote an introduction of Takaha-sensei for the *Mainichi Japanese Newspaper* in Japanese.

May 26

- I really feel that I must learn English again from the start.
- I am thinking of the windmill (which looks like the sail of a yacht).
- Prepared to send the manuscript of English haiku to headquarters.

May 27

- A letter from the Naotsukas. The two of them are doing well, which makes me happy.
- Wrote back to them right away.
- In the *Japan-America Newspaper* there will be an article about me teaching haiku as a tool for colloquial language education. Had Kiyoko phone the Education Department in San Francisco and let them know.
- Had Kiyoko make copies of the article using the copier machine at the Sumitomo bank and mailed them to our members.
- Went to Kei-san's about 10 a.m.

May 28

- No school for Kiyoko because it is Memorial Day, and it's going to be a long weekend.
- Went to a store that sells trophies. Found a good one.
- Kiyoko cut the lawn. I was going to help her, but had to stop due to too much coughing.

June 19

- Kiyoko and I attended the *kukai*.
- Nakajima-san gave us sushi.
- Visited Hisayo-san.

June 20

- Saw Dr. Higuchi.
- Went to San Jose Hospital to have x-rays.
- No letter today.

June 21

- A postcard from Yamagata-san in Frankfurt.
- Typed the *Haiku Journal*.

June 22

- Continued typing the *Haiku Journal*.
- After dinner went to see Toshihiko-san.

July 1

- Went to see Dr. Higuchi. He removed the tube.
- Went to see Yoshimitsu [his brother].
- Kiyoko got tired and went to bed early.

July 2

- It seems to be good to have the tube removed. No sign of drainage.
- English haiku meeting.
- Japanese haiku meeting. Dr. Wiegman came with his wife. Had a great time.

July 7

- Interesting that today is July 7 in 1977, and [it is] the Tanabata Festival (written as the Seventh Evening Festival).
- Went to get my car. At the repair shop I had them drill a hole in the axle of the windmill.
- Went to buy a ball bearing.
- I've been invited to the fifteenth-year celebration of the San Jose branch office of California First Bank[1]. Now I have something to write about. [I can write about] Manager Tsuyama and the head of the branch, Matsuo.
- A letter came from Furukawa Tatsuko-san.
- Thirty dollars came from the San Francisco School District.
- I'm going to work again on the design of the windmill.

[1]California First Bank was originally the Sumitomo Bank. In Yuki Teikei's early years the English language haiku meetings were held in the community room at the San Jose Branch.

July 8

- The design of the windmill came out nicely. Now all I need is to cut cloth for it.
- A bill for my subscription came from Kodansha Publishing Co.

July 15

- Typed the announcement of a general meeting in Canada.
- Borrowed a newspaper on the concentration camp during the war from Akizuki-san. Asked him about the inside story.
- Ordered ten copies of the Kodansha magazine.
- Got photos from the mayor's office. Wrote an article on Aki Bakery.

July 16

- Received a letter from Moritake-san of *San'yō Shinbun*.
- A letter from Uraji-san.
- Sent a letter of request to Takaha-sensei along with the announcement of the All America-Canada Meeting.
- Requested Dr. F[alkowski] to proof it for me.
- Kiyoko and I went to a Chinese restaurant.
- Received a letter from Yamagata-san.

July 17

- The second regular meeting.
- After receiving medals the winner of the March contest got together in JAL Hall. Kiyoko attended.
- Went to see Yamada-san.
- Stopped over to Hisayo-san's. It was about 11:00 p.m.
- Sent the invitation letter for the All America-Canada haiku contest to the printer.

July 18

- Kiyoko went to work.
- Wrote a newspaper article, "Okayama News."
- Started to write articles on English haiku, May-June.
- After dinner visited Takeji-san.
- Wrote to Yamagata-san, Hirakawa-sensei, and Sagara-san.

July 19

- Yōzō-*kun* came. We talked about applying for permanent residence. Then we went to see Toshiko-san and asked him to ask Mr. Kasama about the procedure.
- Started to prepare the English haiku to be sent out.

July 20

- Yōzō-*kun* listened to the tape of the conversation between Mr. Kasama and Toshihiko-san.
- Prepared to send the manuscript of the May-June English haiku.

July 21

- The invitation letter for the haiku contest is done.
- Wrote a letter to Hirakawa-sensei.
- Mailed the invitations out.
- Drafted the invitation for foreign students to get together. Decided to ask Takeda-san for help.
- Wrote an article for the newspaper ("News from Okayama").

July 22

- Dr. Falkowski came to pick up the invitation to the All America-Canada Meeting and stayed for awhile.
- Yōzō-*kun* came.
- Wrote articles for the newspaper ("News from Okayama" and others).
- After dinner went to the hobby shop.

July 23

- The second regular meeting was a great success.
- Kiyoko went out to gather people who are associated with the math contest for the celebration party.
- She came back with new members.

July 24

- Akizuki-san's award party was a great success.
- Went to see Hisayo-san.
- Saw Yukiko in her new place. She prepared lunch for us.

July 25

- A letter of condolence to Motoyama-sensei.
- A realtor came.
- Wrote a letter to Ishimatsu-san.
- Kei-san came with his haiku.

July 26

- A letter from Yamagata-san. Have a great admiration for him.
- A thank-you note to Assistant Counsel Saneoka.
- Had a discussion with Taketa-san about foreign students.
- Yōzō-*kun* came for dinner.

July 27

- Preparing for the publication of *Haiku Journal*.
- Kiyoko went to the copy shop and printed the material.
- We mailed it.

July 28

- Work on the *Haiku Journal* continues.
- Went to Hisayo-san's to watch the movie *Ikiru [To Live]* on her TV.
- Mailed haiku collections in English and Japanese to Japan.

July 29

- A letter from Sagara-san.
- After dinner went to see my brother and had him edit my translation.

July 30

- A letter from Hirakawa-sensei. He told me that next year he plans to attend the All America-Canada Haiku Convention. What a surprise! I reported to Kei-san and Dr. Falkowski right away.
- Kiyoko went to have a haircut.
- Mikami-san came (about the newspaper article).

Aug 1

- Typed the *Haiku Journal*.
- Visited Yoshimitsu.
- During the night I wrote a letter to Takaha-sensei and an article for the newspaper.

Aug 2

- Continued to type the *Haiku Journal*.
- Kiyoko went to work after lunch.
- Mailed a translated version to Takaha-sensei along with a letter.
- Wrote an article about writing haiku outdoors and sent it to the Japan-America Haiku Society.

Aug 3

- Inspector from the City came.
- Typed *Haiku Journal*.
- Kiyoko had a headache so dinner was served at 7:30 p.m.
- Went to Ogura to buy a Japanese magazine.
- On the way home stopped over at Kei-san's.

Aug 4

- Continued to type the *Haiku Journal*.
- A letter from Takaha-sensei came by express mail.
- Takaha-sensei gave me "Merits of Haiku" for *Haiku Journal*.

Aug 5

- Wrote letters to Takaha-sensei, Hirakawa-sensei, and Yamagata-san.
- Work for the *Haiku Journal* is almost done.
- Sent a letter to Kei-san. Stopped over Akizuki-san's with the newspaper to be sent to Okayama. Hirahawa-sensei's visit to America appears difficult.
- When I came home, Tsukiji-san was waiting. I was glad to see him.

Aug 6

- English haiku regular meeting.
- A letter from Hirakawa-sensei.
- Wrote a letter to Higuchi-*kun*.

Aug 7

- A successful meeting of outdoor haiku.
- Akira-san was there too.
- But he went home without stopping at our house.
- Kiyoko and I went to see Yamada-san with the money for the group's lunch and the draft of the group's haiku.
- Visited Hisayo-san.

Aug 8

- A letter from Yamagata-san.
- Finished typing the editorial.

Aug 13

- Went to see Yukiko.
- Then stopped over in Watsonville.
- Joined Hisayo-san's group and enjoyed goodies together at Glen-*chan's* [first son of Kiyoko's sister, Mitsuyo, and her husband, Akira Tao] house.
- Helped Kayoko-san with her house move. Gave her sushi from Ginza.

Aug 14

- Pat [Machmiller] and her husband came. She brought an article for the *Journal*.
- We visited Kayoko-san.
- Went to Hisayo-san's and watched Japanese TV together.

Aug 15

- A letter concerning the motor came from Ikari Shin'ichi-sensei.
- A new person from Texas joined the English haiku [group].
- Drafted a letter to Taniguchi-san.
- After dinner Hisayo-san came to pay her rent.
- Kei-san and his wife came. We talked about Hirakawa's visit to the States.
- Julia Lincoln-sensei mailed her haiku. I was deeply moved.
- I translated some parts of *The Enjoyment of Haiku* [by Shugyo Takaha].

Aug 16

- The magazine *Yukuharu* arrived by airmail.
- The chart of statistics from the Education Committee of Okayama City arrived.
- I was surprised to find that they had not received our statistics chart yet. I wrote letter of complaint right away.
- Wrote a letter to Ikari-san.
- Kiyoko attended a meeting of Japanese [language] teachers.
- Off to grocery shop.

Aug 16

- Wrote to Ikari-san.
- Resent the statistics to the Education Committee.
- Wrote a letter to Taniguchi-san.
- Ōmori-san came.
- Kei-san came. We decided to invite Hirakawa-sensei next year.
- Worked on the translation a little.
- Tanaka-san came with corn, tomatoes, and cucumbers.

Aug 18

- It's been so busy that I'm exhausted.
- I started to prepare the *Haiku Journal*.

Aug 19

- Kiyoko took leave today because she had a headache.
- Went to get groceries.
- Went to see Yoshimitsu [Tokutomi].
- Sent a telegram to Frankie.
- Kei-san and his wife came to see us.
- Wrote to Naotsuka inquiring about private schools.

Aug 20

- Sent an article by the reporter Moritaka titled "Sister City #010" to the main office.
- Kiyoko went shopping.
- Wrote haiku in Japanese.
- A letter [came] from Sagara-san.

Aug 21

- The second regular meeting.
- We were invited to Toshihiko's get-well party. Ten People attended.
- Visited Hisayo-san.
- We have changed the time for inviting Hirakawa-sensei so often, I'm tired of it.

Aug 22

- Wrote a letter to Sagara-san.
- I am disappointed with Maria because she has not sent a card with haiku. I must make it. I could have done it by myself. I said so from the beginning.
- Cooked *tonkatsu* [pork, breaded and fried]. It was delicious but a lot of work.

Aug 23

- Prepared for typing.
- Yōzō-*kun* came early so that he can go to San Francisco to pick up the package.
- About 10:00 a.m. Yōzō-*kun* returned with the package. It contains two thermos bottles and tea—all good quality.
- Sagara-san gave us dried noodles.
- Kiyoko must have had a bad day.

Aug 24

- Finished typing the *Haiku Journal*.
- I am exhausted.
- Went to see Yamada-san.

Aug 25

- Kiyoko and I went to Marihata-san's meeting.
- I made a note about selling high school education to oil-rich countries.

Aug 26

- Retyped part of the note on high school education.
- After dinner visited Yoshimitsu. Somebody sent me a postcard from Russia. I don't know who sent it because there was no name of the sender.
- Someone sent me a publication, "Introduction to High Schools." I am grateful. I called Taketa-san right away.

Aug 27

- I went [somewhere?] to do [something?] for the *Haiku Journal*.
- There was no cooler; it stopped working around 2:00 p.m.

Aug 28

- Kiyoko came home from work about five o'clock so that she can work on the *Haiku Journal*. [Kiyoko did the lay-out.]
- Glen-*chan* came to see us. He says that he might be able to disprove Faraday's rule. We discussed the electricity for March 17. Glen-*chan* was excited in anticipation.
- Went to Dr. Falkowski's to have him look at the *Haiku Journal*.

Sept 11

- Dr. Wiegman came.
- Glen-*chan* came.
- Kiyoko went out to finish the *Haiku Journal*.
- Went grocery shopping at Safeway.
- Glen-*chan* came and we talked for a long time.
- Kiyoko went to see Hisayo-san.
- I said "Life is love." "Love is life," said Glen-*chan*. Life without love? [Love] makes things meaningful. I told Glen-*chan* there is no point in living if there is not love in our life. It's 10:40 p.m.

Sept 12

- Translated Dr. Weigman's letter.
- Had a meeting to discuss the invitation to be sent to Hirakawa-sensei.
- Sayoko-san called.

Sept 13

- I finished the translation of Dr. Wiegman's letter.
- Finished the report on the mathematics competition for the newspaper.

Sept 14

- Dr. Wiegman came.
- [illegible]
- Translated Toshihiko-san's work.
- Wrote a letter to Miki-sensei about the mathematics competition.
- Wrote letters to Sayoko-san and Junko-san.
- Neussia Trashawn da Kumari—
    Intelligent woman who is most beautiful in the morning like sunrise on water. [original in English]

Sept 27

- Finished typing Toshihiko-san's paper.
- I gave it to him after dinner.
- Kiyoko came home after 8:00 p.m. due to the amount of work she had to do.

Sept 28

- Kiyoko finished the haiku manuscript and brought it to me in the early afternoon.
- Telephone call from Naotsuka.
- Sent a letter to Naotsuka.
- Mailed the haiku manuscript.

Sept 29

- I am anxiously awaiting the *Haiku Journal*.
- I am nervous.
- Sue (the realtor) came to see us.
- Yōzō-*kun's* car had some trouble.
- He took a taxi to school.
- Later we took a taxi to pick him up.

Sept 30

- Finally the *Haiku Journal* is published. It is gorgeous! I am deeply moved. I'm grateful to Kiyoko. We stuck to it . . . our tenaciousness brought this result. A letter came from Yamagata-san.
- Junko-san came around noon. Four of us went to lunch. Junko-san invited us.
- We will send a copy of *Haiku Journal* to Junko-san. For now we gave her *The Enjoyment of Haiku* by Takaha-sensei.
- We went to Kuwata-san's in San Francisco together with Imamura-san's group from the Japanese Language Association. Afterwards we went with them for the first time to the Bar Shinjuku.

Oct 1

- Kiyoko went to the Japanese School to teach.
- Susan came.
- We all went to the regular meeting for English haiku.
- I distributed the *Haiku Journal* to the members.
- To prepare for Hirakawa-sensei's visit next year I am teaching one Japanese phrase a day. Today I taught "Hello, everybody!"
- In order to improve the *Haiku Journal,* I proposed that we create a number of groups in charge of public relations, introduction of books, etc. [My proposal] was approved.

Oct 2

- I attended the Robert Frost Chapter of the Poet's Association.
- I talked about the poems of Haku Raku Ten.
- Kiyoko went shopping with Yōzō-*kun* and his mother.
- I asked my wife to cook Chinese noodles.
- [illegibile]
- Wrote to Takaha-sensei; also mailed him the *Haiku Journal*.

Oct 3

- My birthday—a letter from Naotsuka. It made me cry.
- Fukaya-*kun* sent me a sculpture of a bear. I had my best birthday.
- The complete run of *Haiku Journal* has arrived.
- Together with Kiyoko I went to Los (Gatos? Altos?) to teach math.

Oct 4

- Corrected a misprint in the *Haiku Journal* with the help of Mrs. Naotsuka. I feel good because it's all done.

Oct 5

- Picked up my car and went shopping—first to Levitz [furniture store], then to Orchard Supply.
- I took Mrs. Naotsuka.
- I stopped at Ogura and bought a Japanese magazine.
- Bought a few things at Dobashi [in Japantown].
- Left my new magazine at Dobashi.
- Ōmori-san came.

Oct 6

- Dr. Falkowski came to pick up the *Haiku Journal*.
- Went to Dobashi to pick up the Japanese magazine that I left there yesterday.
- Sayoko-san came unexpectedly with Nō Seiei-san and his wife. Enjoyed the sushi that she brought.

Oct 11

- Prepared to send the manuscript for July and August to Japan.
- I don't feel well.
- Kiyoko went to Yamada-san's for a haircut.
- A letter from Yamagata-san to tell me that the *Haiku Journal* had arrived.

Oct 12

- Wrote a thank-you note to Fukaya-*kun*'s daughter.
- Practiced calligraphy.
- Kiyoko attended a company party.
- I went to Yoshimitsu's.
- Wrote a letter to the Counsel General.

Oct 13

- I have a headache.
- Kiyoko is working very late.

Oct 14

- Felt ill all day.
- Kiyoko is working late again.
- Asked Yōzō-*kun* to bring me some medicine.
- Went to see Kayoko-san.
- Started making the package of English haiku to be sent to Japan.

Oct 27

- One person in Arizona wants to become a member.
- Had Hisayo-san check the translation of the mathematics problems.
- [illegible]

Oct 28

- One person in Sunnyvale sent an application for membership.
- A letter from Tennessee about membership.
- Answered the above.
- Wrote a letter to the Education Committee in Okayama City about mathematics problems.
- Went to Hisayo's to pick up the math papers that I had asked her to check.
- Wrote letters to Dr. Kusler and Dr. Roan. Sent them the *Haiku Journal*.
- Also to Yōzō-*kun*, *Haiku Journal* and a letter.

Oct 29

- Kiyoko went to teach at the Japanese School.
- In the evening we went to see Sayoko-san.

Oct 30

- We went shopping at Eastridge [Shopping Mall] with Yōzō-*kun*. [When we left,] I had to wait in front for more than an hour and a half while they looked for the car. I am amazed at their lack of a sense of direction.
- Went to Jade for dinner.
- Stopped over at Hisayo-san's.

Nov 1

- Rewrote the letter to Hirakawa-sensei.
- After dinner Kiyoko went to type up the English haiku.
- Went to my brother's, but he was out. Had a discussion with Eric and Kenny [Kiyoshi's brother's sons] about guns.

Nov 2

- [First sentence is about Yōzō-*kun;* the rest is illegible.] I could not hear anything. I just tried to see everything.
- Asked Ōmori-san to come to Yōzō-*kun's* house. About 1:30 p.m. [something] was delivered so I asked Ōmori-san to mail it.
- We went to Yamada-san's in the evening. Mrs. Yamada is so nice. They have a beautiful garden.
- I mailed the *Haiku Journal* to three people.
- I must ask Takaha-sensei to speed up the translation.
- I am anxious to work on the flying saucer.

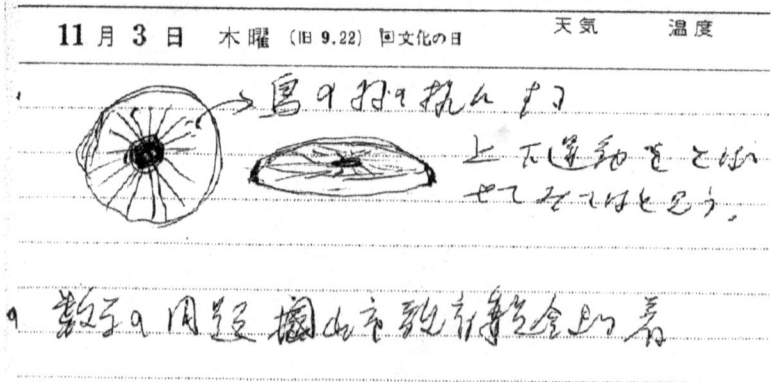

Nov 3

- [Notes on the illustration, previous page:] Make it like a bird's feather. Let it move up and down, maybe.
- Received questions on mathematics from Okayama City Education Committee.

Nov 4

- Went to Yōzō-*kun* and waited for the delivery of his new desk. It came about 1:00 p.m.
- Went to [illegible] to give them the *Haiku Journal*.
- Went to the Sumitomo Bank to get the key for Kiyoko.
- Went to Hisayo-san's to ask her to translate the math exercise.

Nov 5

- Today is the English haiku meeting.
- Dr. Falkowski announced that Junko-san donated $500 to the group. We discussed the plan[1] of inviting Hirakawa-sensei to come next year.

[1] Mr. Hirakawa, the President of the Yukuharu Haiku Society with branches in Tokyo, Hawaii, and San Jose did, in fact, come in September 1978. The two Yukuharu groups, English and Japanese, of San Jose hosted a joint dinner for him at the LeBaron Hotel (now gone) on First Street in San Jose. During this time of preparation for Mr. Hirakawa's arrival, tensions between the Japanese and English language groups must have been exacerbated. The Tokutomis never indicated that there were problems, but immediately after Mr. Hirakawa left San Jose, they made the decision to leave the Yukuharu Haiku Society and become independent. They renamed the society the Yuki Teikei Haiku Society.

Nov 6

- Hiromichi-san's [Kiyoshi's sister's husband] retirement party.
- We celebrated with Toshihiko-san's family and Yoshimitsu-san's family at the restaurant Gifu.

Nov 7

- Day of calligraphy. After dinner we went to Gismon-san's (?) house. On the way we picked up Herse-sans (?) and took them home after the gathering. I really enjoyed being with these people.

Nov 8

- We were invited to the dinner party introducing the new Sumitomo Branch Chief.

Nov 21

- Taught calligraphy today. On the way back I stopped at Ichikawa-san's and picked up the selected math exercises.
- Since there was no deposit in the English haiku account, I went to the Sumitomo bank to check on it.
- Wrote haiku in the car while waiting for Kiyoko.
- Went to Ogura to buy books.
- Went to Okamoto with some money.

Nov 22

- Wrote to the Education Committee in Okayama.
- Sent a thank-you note to Sagara-san. They had sent us lilies.
- Yōzō-*kun* came.
- Went to see Toshihiko-san.
- Had a quarrel with Kiyoko.

Nov 23

- Sagara-san sent us *kasutera* pound cake[1].
- Wrote an announcement of English haiku for the New Year's edition.

[1] *Kasutera* pound cake was introduced to Japan by Portuguese missionaries in the Muromachi Period (1336-1573).

Nov 24

- Thanksgiving Day. Nothing special.
- Went to see Toshio-san.
- Junko-san gave us some pomegranates.
- Ōmori-san gave us *akebi*. It's called *mube* or *uke*.

Nov 25

- A letter from Junko-san.
- Kiyoko's article on the Calligraphy Club is in the newspaper.
- Yukiko came home with a turkey.
- All of went to see Grandmother [Kiyoshi's mother].
- Stopped by my sister's [Mitsuye Hoshino]. Gave condolences to Hiromichi-san [Mitsuye's husband] for his brother's passing.

Nov 26

- Went to San Francisco with Kiyoko to buy a book on calligraphy. Bought a brush too.
- Tanaka-san came with his haiku. He wants me to edit it for submission to *Nichibei Newspaper* [in San Francisco].
- A letter from Yamagata-san. He is very pleased with the *Haiku Journal*.
- Letters from Masayoshi-san [Kiyoko's youngest brother] and Sumie-san [his wife].
- Kiyoko made *saba-zushi* [bite-sized raw mackerel with vinegared rice]. It was delicious.

Nov 27

- Took *Haiku Saijiki* with illustrations to Yoshii-san.
- Made sushi with mackerel, and we had dinner together at Hisayo-san's.
- Ōmori-san came. Kōchi-san might join the calligraphy group.

Nov 28

- Wrote letters to Sumie-san and Masayoshi-san.
- Contacted Collins, [Roberta] Stuart, and [Ethyl] Dunlap because they have not paid their dues.
- Thank you note to [illegible].

Dec 13

- Wrote Season's Greetings
- Inquiries on the English haiku contest increased.
- Yōzō-*kun* came early, ate, and left.

Dec 14

- Started the calligraphy club. Had Ōmori-san pick me up. Four people gathered—Ōmori-san, Miyazaki-san, [illegible], and me. The work will start the second Wednesday of the New Year.
- Busy with greeting cards.
- Went to Ogura to buy a Japanese magazine. Bought a cup of noodles from Dobashi.

Dec 15

- Busy writing New Year's greeting cards. Almost done and posted.

Dec 16

- Yōzō-*kun's* mother came.
- Yukiko came home.
- We went to Jade for Chinese food.
- A rainy day.
- Yukiko left.

Dec 21

- So many inquiries about the English haiku contest. I am surprised.

Dec 22

- Kiyoko came home early due to a cold.
- Tsukiji-san came with the mathematics questionnaire.
- A letter from Akaboshi-san in Japan. He wants to become a member of our Calligraphy Club!
- Prepared a noodle dish and took it to Yōzō-*kun*.
- Sent a letter to Yamagata-san.
- A letter and a gift from Akizuki-san. (I must send something in return—I have not done anything for them this year.)
- Magazine *Haiku* arrived.
- A gift from Sayoko-san and Junko-san.

Dec 23

- A letter from Yamagata-san.
- *Nemunoki* magazine arrived.
- Visited Yōzō-*kun*.
- Visited Ōmori-san and practiced calligraphy. I was surprised to see everybody signed names so beautifully.
- Kiyoko was sick in bed all day.

Dec 24

- Christmas Eve.
- Couldn't go anywhere because Kiyoko was sick. Phoned Kanemoto-san and Mr. Wedenvich to decline their invitation.
- Yukiko came home very late.

Dec 25

- Christmas.
- Susan came early in the morning carrying a turkey.
- We all enjoyed it. Yōzō-*kun* and his family were here with us.
- I'm concerned with Yukiko's weight.

Dec 26

- Glen-*chan* and his family came. I told him about 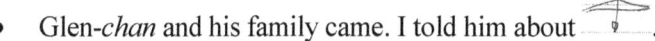 .
- After Glen-*chan* and his group left, we went to house and stayed till about 5:00 p.m.

"We think we are the most important being. But don't forget that we have parents, and we have others all around us. Without others we don't exist nor have we reason to be alive. Others are as important as we are."

Dec 27

- Wrote back to Nagata-sensei. (He wrote me a very courteous letter.)

Dec 28

- Naotsuka came from Japan.
- Kiyoko and I went shopping this morning.
- Four of went to the Chinese restaurant.
- They [Naotsukas probably] bought me a Chinese dictionary and a calligraphy book. I am grateful.
- Kiyoko's mother sent us tea.

www.ingramcontent.com/pod-product-compliance
Lightning Source LLC
Chambersburg PA
CBHW071733040426
42446CB00012B/2342